OFF-ROADING VEHICLES

JEEPS®

TAMRA B. ORR

Mitchell Lane
PUBLISHERS

Parent and Caregiver Tips for Creating Nonfiction Readers

The high-interest topics in the *Off-Roading Vehicles* series are sure to get your young reader excited about reading nonfiction. While exploring a fascinating subject, your reader will be introduced to new concepts, facts, ideas, and vocabulary.

Tips for Reading Nonfiction

Talk about Nonfiction

Explain that nonfiction books provide facts about real-world topics. When readers read nonfiction, they gain a rich understanding of the world. They build background knowledge that provides a foundation for learning and academic success.

Look at the Parts

This book contains the following helpful features. Share the purpose of each feature with your reader.

Photos, Captions, and Graphic Aids
The photos, captions, charts, maps, and other graphic aids in nonfiction texts contain a wealth of information. Help your reader identify different ways information can be displayed. A special feature, "A Closer Look," puts the spotlight on learning through images.

Sidebars
These extra tidbits of information help satisfy readers' curiosity and expand their knowledge.

Table of Contents
Located at the front of the book, this list shows the big ideas within the text and the page numbers where they can be found.

Glossary
Located at the back of the book, the glossary defines key words and phrases that are related to the topic. These words and phrases can be found in the text in **bold** type.

Comprehension Questions (Fact Check)
Multiple-choice questions help readers self-check to make sure they understand what they read.

Index
Located at the back of the book, the index is an alphabetical list of topics and the page numbers where they can be found.

With a little help and guidance, your reader will be on their way to enjoying and learning from nonfiction books.

Mitchell Lane
PUBLISHERS

mitchelllanepub.com

2001 SW 31st Avenue
Hallandale, FL 33009

First Edition, 2026.
Author: Tamra B. Orr
Designer: Kathy Walsh
Editor: Tricia Hoffman

Series: Off-Roading Vehicles
Title: Jeeps / by Tamra B. Orr

Hallandale, FL : Mitchell Lane Publishers, [2026]

Library bound ISBN: 979-8-89260-567-0
Paperback ISBN: 979-8-89260-596-0
eBook ISBN: 979-8-89260-571-7

Photo Credits
Adobe: background, miloje; Alamy: p24 & 29, Andy Soloman; p26 & 29, ZUMA Press Inc; p7 & 28, kevin cable; p19 & 28, Vilijam Cirkovic; p5, Rubens Alarcon; p8, Barry Crook; p9, Everett Collection Inc; p 10, Wirestock, Inc.; p11, John Muggenborg; p12, Retro AdArchives; p13, Edwin Remsberg; p14, Rob Scorah; p18, Edwin Remsberg; p23, UPI; p28, Rubens Alarcon; Shutterstock: Cover, Title pg, p20 & 29, Pan_photo; p5, Metha1819; p6, Cavan-Images; p15, Mike Mareen; p 16, BNFWork; p17, Gary Le Feuvre; p22, Athenaeum creations; p25, LisaCarter

Contents

A Famous Four-Wheeler

RAAARRRR!

Uh oh. What's that behind you? A dinosaur!

Buckle up.

Slam the gas pedal.

And go—fast!

If a Tyrannosaurus rex is chasing you, you're going to want a reliable vehicle! When movie director Steven Spielberg needed one that was dinosaur-tough, he chose a 1992 Wrangler YJ Sahara Jeep®.

It tumbled over. It fell out of trees. It was crunched and bitten. But the Jeep kept the *Jurassic Park* heroes safe.

JURASSIC PARK

Jeeps have been used in movies and on television for years. Along with the many different movies in the *Jurassic Park* franchise, they have appeared in everything from one of the *Fast and Furious* movies to the character of Sarge in Disney's *Cars*.

Jeeps have been part of history for almost 75 years. While they aren't currently needed for protection from hungry dinosaurs, they are a great off-roading vehicle that promises a lot of fun.

IT'S OFFICIAL

In 2016, April 4 was declared National Jeep 4x4 Day. This date was chosen because of its numerical format—April 4, or 4/4, represents the four-wheel drive vehicles.

A Long History

The name *jeep* first appeared in the early 1940s. The Army needed a strong, sturdy vehicle that could quickly move supplies and soldiers from place to place. They designed a powerful 550-pound (250-kg), four-door vehicle.

This vehicle was designed to go on roads and across rough **terrain**. It could carry up to six people, along with weapons such as **mortars** and machine guns. Its powerful engine could go up steep slopes and across shallow streams.

ALL ABOARD!

During World War II, some jeeps were fitted with wagon wheels so they could move supplies on train tracks.

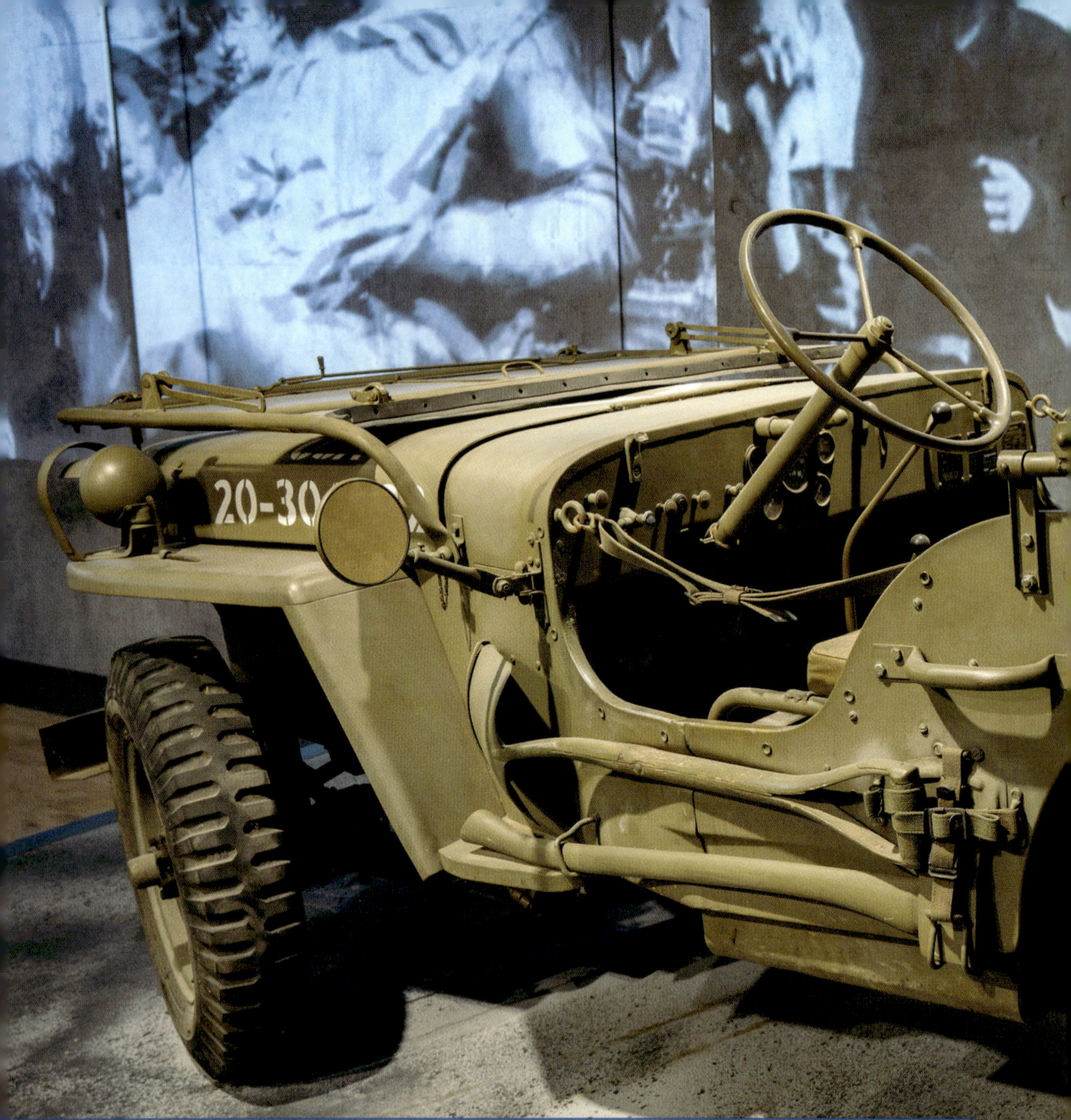

Where the jeep got its name is still a mystery. Some believe it was based on the Army calling it a "general purpose" vehicle. When "GP" was said quickly, it sounded like "jeep."

Others believe the jeep was named after Eugene the Jeep, a magical character that appeared in *Popeye* comics in the mid-1930s. This brave and daring character wasn't afraid to go anywhere or do anything—which later became Jeep's official **motto**.

A PURPLE HEART RECIPIENT

In 1943, the jeep was one of the first vehicles to arrive at two important battles of World War II. Even after being hit with bullets, it kept going, earning it a **Purple Heart**.

From jeep to Jeep

Even though World War II ended in the mid-1940s, jeeps kept coming. The company making them thought that **civilians** would enjoy them for **recreational** reasons. They were right. During the 1950s, seven styles were released, and the name Jeep became a registered trademark. Now, instead of *jeeps*, they're *Jeeps*!

ACROSS THE GLOBE

By the end of the 1950s, Jeeps were being manufactured in 30 different countries and sold in more than 150 countries.

The Cherokee and Wrangler

Two of the most popular styles of Jeep are the Cherokee and the Wrangler. First developed in the 1960s and 1970s, they quickly began winning awards for the best four-wheelers on the market.

JEEP CHEROKEE

The two models are similar, but have differences. The Jeep Cherokee is a traditional four-door **SUV**. The Jeep Wrangler can have two or four doors and a soft or hard top. Both types have 4x4 systems with powerful engines and thousands of pounds of **towing power**.

JEEP WRANGLER

CHANGING OWNERSHIP

Over the years, Jeep has been owned by many companies. Today, they are made by Stellantis. In the past, they were manufactured by Chrysler, Renault, Ford, and the American Motor Corp.

A Distinct Design

One of the most recognizable parts of a Jeep is its front steel grille. Those seven slots are known by all off-roading fans. But the grille did not always look like that.

The original jeeps in 1940 had between 10 and 16 slots in the grille. As the ownership of the vehicle changed, so did the grille. Ford put nine-slot grilles on their model in 1942. Finally, in 1945, Jeep grilles were changed to the seven slots known today.

4291853
U S A

Going Off-Road

Although Jeeps might be seen driving around town, they were meant for outdoor adventures. Some of the off-roading activities Jeep owners enjoy most are mudding and rock crawling.

Mudding is messy fun, but it's easy for tires to get stuck in the mud. Keep gears low. If the Jeep starts slipping, move the steering wheel back and forth.

SAFETY FIRST

Remember, you must be 16 years old and have a driver's license to drive a Jeep.

Rock crawling is when off-roaders drive across boulders, rock piles, or other very difficult terrain. It should be taken slowly with low gears. Going over sharp, hard rocks can damage a Jeep, so caution is important! Some owners modify their Jeeps to protect their vehicles.

These "mods" include skid plates, or slabs of metal that protect the Jeep's **drivetrain**, **shock mounts**, and gas tank. Some off-roaders invest in special LED headlights to illuminate trails. Owners can also purchase a rooftop tent so they can go camping.

A Few "Easter Eggs"

Take a close look at Jeeps—they might have a few surprises for you. Over the years, manufacturers have had fun putting "Easter eggs," or hidden images and features, in their various models. These include:

- √ A silhouette of Big Foot in the rear window
- √ A spider near the gas cap
- √ Mud spatter on the **tachometer**
- √ A pair of flip flops on the windshield wipers
- √ A Loch Ness monster on the rear window
- √ A seven-slot grille on the headlights

JEEPS AT THE WHITE HOUSE

Even U.S. presidents like Jeeps! Ronald Reagan was known for driving one on the White House grounds. In 2021, Joe Biden took an electric model for a spin.

Prepare for the Future

Although it may be a few years before you're ready to go off-roading behind the wheel, you can have fun practicing and planning for that day. You can watch videos about mudding and rock crawling. You can read about Jeeps and their long history.

You might have a family member or friend who owns a Jeep that you could take a ride in. There are even kid-sized ride-on Jeeps that you can buy and drive.

A NEW RECORD

In 2015, the world record for the longest parade of Jeeps was set in Butler, Pennsylvania, when 2,420 Jeeps drove in single file through the city.

Jeeps in Action

Want to see Jeeps in action? Check out the Jeepers Jamboree. For more than 70 years, Jeep families have come to the Rubicon Trail over the Sierra Nevada Mountain Range. More than 100 drivers travel the 7.5-mile (12-km) trail full of huge rocks, deep mud, and amazing scenery.

Driving a Jeep used to mean being in the Army. Today, it means having an amazing off-roading vehicle that's just waiting for someone to turn the key. Start the adventure!

THE CAPITAL

Ouray, Colorado, is considered the Jeep Capital of the World. It offers some amazing adventures for Jeep owners of all ages.

A Closer Look

Does this *Jurassic Park* Jeep really exist?

It can! In 2023, Jeep offered customers a package of Jurassic Park *decals and logos to add to their vehicle's doors, front fenders, and hood.*

Where are these Jeeps?

These drivers are taking their Jeeps off the road and on to the beach! Thousands of Jeeps take to the sand for Jeep Beach, a two-week event held each year in Daytona Beach, Florida.

How will this Jeep get clean?

Removing mud after your mudding adventure can be the hardest part, so using a high-pressure washer is best. Also, try to wash the Jeep as soon as you can. Mud hardens quickly, especially in warm weather. Hardened mud can feel like concrete!

Is rock crawling tough on the vehicle?

Yes. Rock crawling can damage a Jeep if precautions aren't taken. Metal can get bent, oil pans can get smashed, and tires can be cut on sharp edges.

What is this boy doing?

He's driving a child-sized Jeep in a parade. You might see these vehicles along the route of a holiday parade in your area. Drivers don't even need a driver's license!

How much do Jeeps cost?

A Jeep's price tag can depend on several factors, including body style and trim. They usually cost between $30,000 and $90,000.

Glossary

civilian (suh-VIL-yuhn)
a person who is not in the military

drivetrain (drive-trayn)
the parts of a vehicle concerned with generating power and sending it to the wheels

mortar (MOR-tur)
a short cannon that throws shells

motto (MAH-toh)
a statement used as the purpose of a person or product

Purple Heart (PUR-puhl hahrt)
honor given to American soldiers who are injured during combat

recreational (rek-ree-AY-shuh-nuhl)
of or relating to recreation, fun, or relaxing activities

SUV
sport utility vehicle

shock mounts (shahk mounts)
a mechanical fastener that protects from vibrations

tachometer (ta-KOM-i-ter)
an instrument for measuring speed

terrain (tuh-RAYN)
a section of land

towing power (TOH-ing POU-ur)
the maximum amount of weight a vehicle can tow when pulling a trailer

Fact Check

1. You have to have a _____ in order to drive a Jeep.
   A. drivetrain B. driver's license C. tachometer
2. The first jeeps were intended for _____.
   A. the military B. civilians C. racecar drivers
3. Today, Jeeps are made by ______.
   A. the Army B. Ford C. Stellantis
4. Rock-crawling should be done _____.
   A. quite slowly B. in high gear C. on the highway

Answers: 1. B, 2. A, 3. C, 4. A

Further Reading

Abdo, Kenny. *Jeep Wranglers (Off Road Vehicles)*. Fly!, 2017.

Chandler, Matt. *The Tech Behind Off-Road Vehicles (Tech on Wheels)*. Capstone Global Library, 2020.

Hayes, Jackson. *Ford Bronco Badlands vs. Jeep Wrangler Rubicon (Epic Motor Matchups)*. Gray Duck Creative Works, 2021.

Riggins, Shari. *Jacey the Jeep*. Covenant Books, 2021.

On the Internet

Beginners Guide to Jeeping with Kids
dirtroadfamilyadventures.com/beginners-guide-to-jeeping-with-kids/
This article focuses on how families can enjoy Jeep adventures together, including helpful tips and details about safety.

Jeep Facts for Kids
kids.kiddle.co/Jeep
Explore detailed information on all kinds of Jeeps, including different models and the history of Jeeps.

What Age are Jeeps Suitable for Children?
us.tobbi.com/what-age-are-jeeps-kids-suitable-for-children/
This site walks through the different types of toy and regular Jeeps that are available for ages 0 to 13, and also includes information on safety and quality.

Index

About the Author

Tamra B. Orr is a mom, wife, grandmother, and full-time writer and author living in the beautiful all-terrain Pacific Northwest. She lives in the state where there is a huge Jeep Jamboree each June. This two-day event brings hundreds of Jeep drivers to the area. A graduate of Ball State University, she has written more than 750 nonfiction and educational books for readers of all ages and loves her job. It gives her the chance to learn about something new—and then share that information with readers of all ages—every single day.